birthdays and birth signs

in lace

birthdays and birth signs

in lace

Edited by Bridget M. Cook

B T Batsford Ltd, London

Publisher's Acknowledgement
The publishers would like to acknowledge the contribution of Bridget M. Cook to this book, in both its overall compilation and co-ordination, and the production of the prickings and working diagrams.

Liz Tibbetts contributed greatly to the concept, and the publishers would like to acknowledge her involvement.

First published 1997

© B.T. Batsford Ltd 1997

ISBN 0 7134 7788 1

Designed by Peter Higgins
Printed in Hong Kong

A CIP record for this title is available from the British Library

Published by
B T Batsford Ltd
583 Fulham Road
London SW6 5BY

Contents

List of contributors

Liz Tibbetts:	Signs of the Zodiac Brooches
Gerlinde Simon:	Brooch for a 21st Birthday

Bridget M. Cook:	Birthday Coasters
	  18th
	  25th
	  40th
	Cake Mat - 50 and not out!
	30th Anniversary Handkerchief Corner

Dorothy McComb:	Capricorn Table Coaster
Radmila Zuman:	Sagittarius Picture
Jeanette S.J. van Ord:	A Quarter Century of Love
Lesley Thomas:	Life Begins at 40 Cake Band
Pat Milne:	21st Birthday Presentation Handkerchief
Gil Dye:	Picture Frame 25th and 50th Birthday Motifs

Helene Schou:	Table Coasters
	  Scorpio
	  Pisces
	  Gemini
	  Capricorn

Inge Skovgaard:	Pisces Cravat

The international colour-coding system

The drawings for all the projects in the Batsford Lace Library have been prepared using the colour-coding system that has been established as the world standard:

Red: Clothstitch and twist (cross, twist, cross, twist) Wholestitch and twist

Purple: Clothstitch (cross, twist, cross) Wholestitch

Green: Halfstitch (cross, twist)

Yellow: The movement of an individual thread. This colour is frequently used to indicate the movement of a gimp thread.

Blue: A two-pair plait

Black: A coarse pair is a mixed threaded pair with one thread thicker than its partner, which is the same thread as used in the rest of the lace. This pair outlines the lace.

Helpful hints for presentation

Mounting lace onto fabric

Select a cloth of a similar weight and feel as the work when mounting the lace.

To attach the lace choose the thread used to create the work or one slightly thicker (and therefore stronger), especially if it is very fine. Choose a needle compatible with the work. A very fine oversewing stitch is the simplest when attaching lace to an existing hem.

Be warned that ready-made handkerchiefs and traycloths may not be truly square or rectangular. The lace should be made to fit the longest side and it can be then gently eased onto any slightly shorter sides. Care should be taken when mounting onto fabric without a hem that the pinholes lie correctly on the weave of the material. For straight edges it is sensible to draw a thread. Pin and tack carefully and attach into every hole of the footside using mock hem stitch, four-sided stitch or a triangular stitch.

On completion of the sewing cut carefully close to the edge. For extra strength and for particularly fine work do not cut too closely. Either roll carefully and whip back the raw edge or, alternatively, make a second row of four-sided stitch. Use a backing of coloured paper for very fine lace and for attaching to net. This will keep the lace in its correct shape and will help to identify the holes for sewing. Pin and tack the lace right-side-down on the paper and then tack the net on top. Oversew the lace to the net, including any motifs inside the border. Then remove the paper and cut the net close to the edge.

Mounting in frames or purpose-bought mounts

Use a small scrape of clear-drying general-purpose PVA adhesive dabbed onto the back of a denser part of the work. Secure the work to the chosen backing material and assemble the frame. Glass, perspex and thick clear PVC film (acetate) are all suitable to protect the work.

Antique frames can often be found and one should always be on the lookout for these. They can be very satisfying and particularly suitable for lace work. Modern purpose-made craft mounts can be in the form of trinket boxes, jewellery, frames, key rings and powder compacts. They all have different methods of holding the craft work in place but all should come with clear instructions.

For paperweights, wedge with a spacer of thick dark card, under the lace and its backing, if needed to keep the work from slipping, and finish with a disc of sticky-backed suede vinyl.

Special mounts can be expensive but most designs can be mounted just as effectively on ready-cut cards. Many shapes and sizes are available including bookmarks, gift tags and shapes of sufficient size for large pictures. The best will have a ready-cut aperture behind which the design is fixed with a double fold of card so that the fixing of the work is obscured. For a professional finish protect the work with a thin clear PVC sheet cut slightly larger than the aperture and glued to the back of it.

Different backings of card or fabric can create different results and add an ingredient to the gift or occasion. Silk or velvet is luxurious, but beware of deep pile for fine work as the lace can sometimes move with the pile if handled.

Other ideas for mounting lace

For a permanent and durable finish iron on clear protective coverings as used for covering pressed flowers, in satin matt finish. This seals directly onto most flat surfaces and is ideal for finishing wood mounts such as clock faces, boxes or small wood blocks for making brooches or pendants.

Lace made with thicker thread does not necessarily need to be mounted or covered. Mats and bookmarks can be stiffened with a weak solution of starch or ironed with spray starch. In order to avoid squashing the work place the right side down onto a soft pad and press lightly. A special preparation, such as the stiffener used to make roller blinds, can be used to stick and seal lace to a backing fabric or to stiffen the piece from a light finish to one that is rock-hard. In this way small pieces of work can be stiffened to make jewellery. In order to avoid clogging or opaqueness use thinned and apply several coats until the desired stiffness is obtained. Stiffeners are also required for any 3-D work or lace that is to be hung. This can include a wall or window hanging as it also protects the lace from dust and dirt.

Many of the mounts and fixings can be found in craft suppliers', model shops, florists' and stationers'. Seek out something different, and be inventive in order to create that special lace gift for family or friends.

Signs of the Zodiac

Liz Tibbetts UK

All the designs in this Zodiac section are suitable for setting in small frames and jewellery.

Thread: 120/2 Brok cotton
Coarse thread: Coats traditional soft cotton

Taurus

Make the face first and then add the horns.

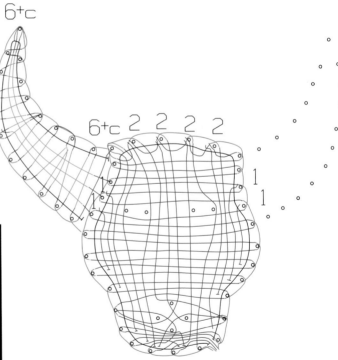

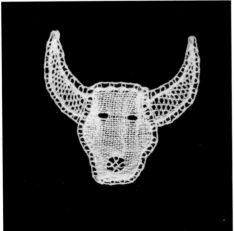

Gemini

Make one, then the other in the same manner.
Join together with sewings where touching.

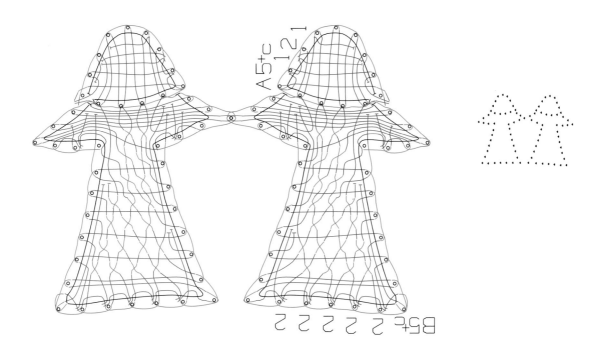

Cancer

When sewing the pincer and legs into the body,
leave the threads long until all have been
completed for one side before cutting close
to the work.

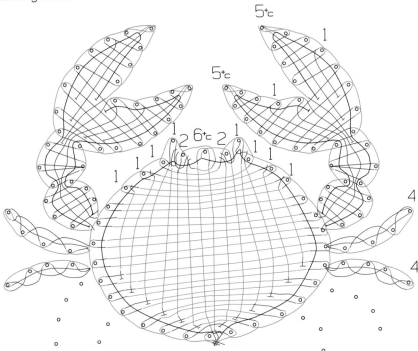

Leo

The rib is worked first to form the features and
then the pillow is turned through 180 degrees
to work the face.

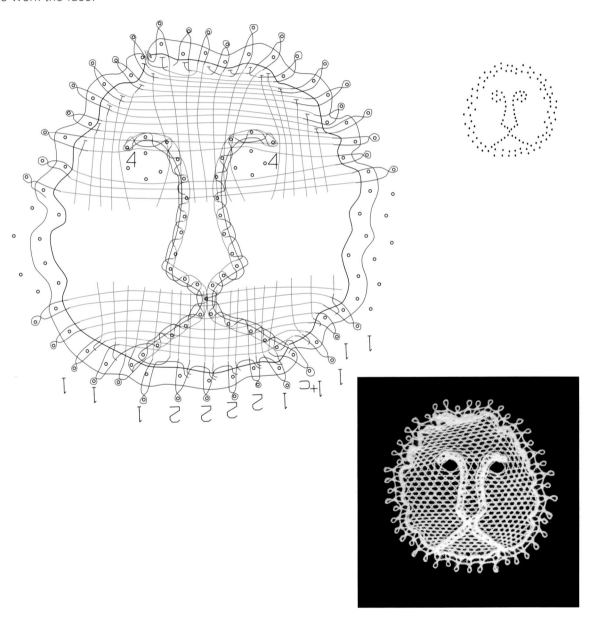

Virgo

When working the rib for the hair, keep the pinholes on the outside of the curve, changing sides as necessary.

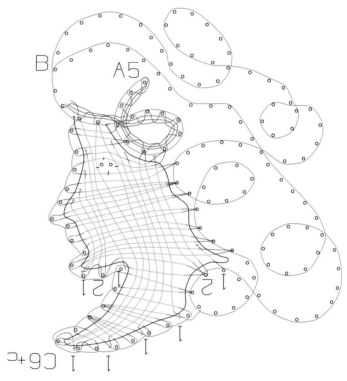

14

Libra

The scales are joined to the stand with halfstitch
bars or plaits. Remember to keep two pairs out
of the tying back at the end of each scale for
the return pair.

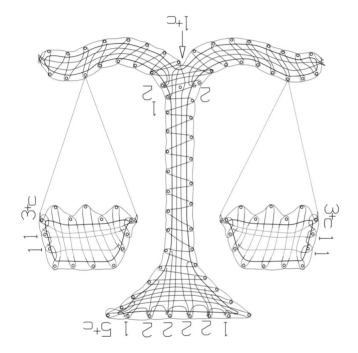

Scorpio

When sewing the pincer and legs into the body,
leave the threads long until all have been
completed for one side before cutting close
to the work.

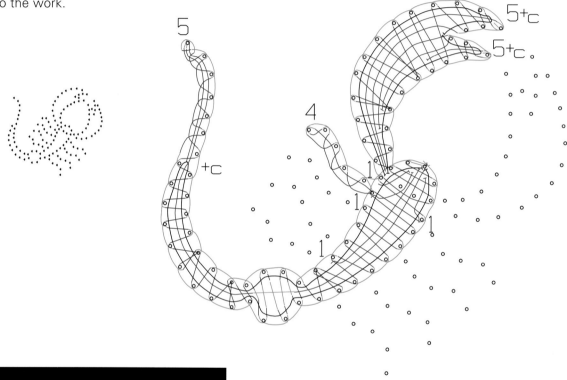

16

Sagittarius

Keep two pairs out of the bunching and tying at
the end of the bow, ready to make a halfstitch
bar or plait to form the string of the bow.

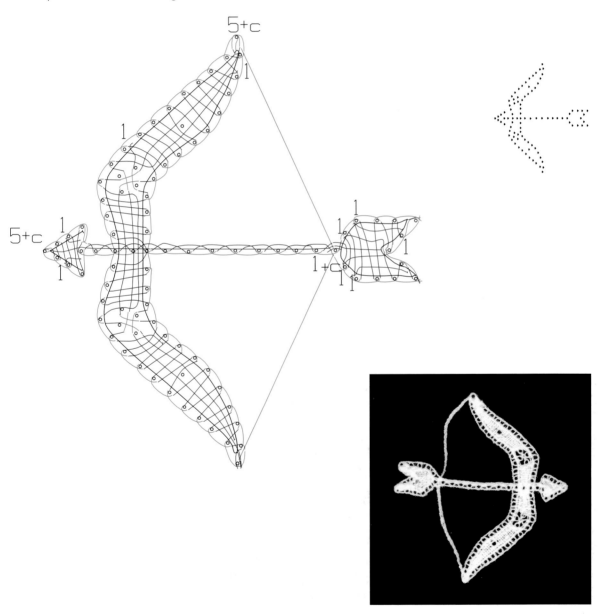

Capricorn

It is not necessary to work the little twisted
veins in the neck exactly as in the photographs,
as long as enough are included at random
to break up the solid effect of the clothstitch.

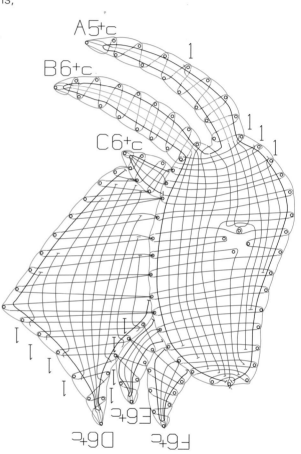

Aquarius

In the twisted section, pull up well several times
during and at the end of each row, so helping
to keep them correctly aligned.

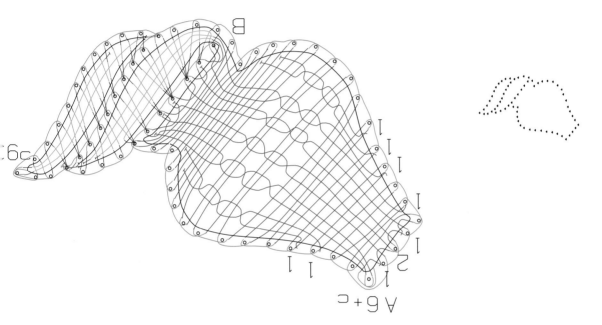

Pisces

Make one, then the other in the same manner.
Join with sewings where touching.

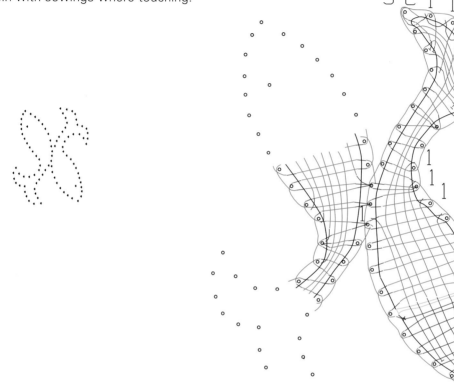

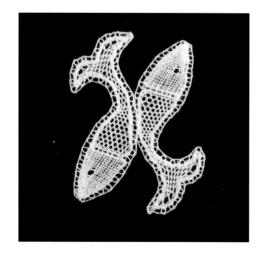

Aries

The holes in the horn are twisted pinholes.
After completing each row of these, tie one of
the more central pairs of downrights and pull
up gently. This will help to keep the cloth in
the correct shape in subsequent rows.

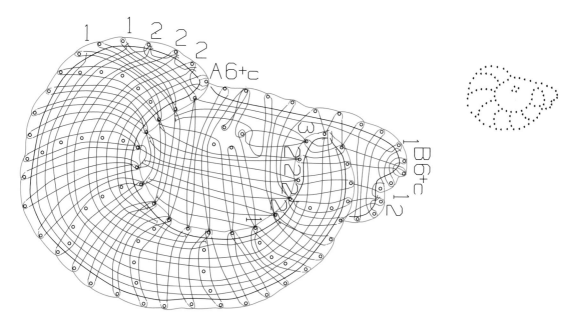

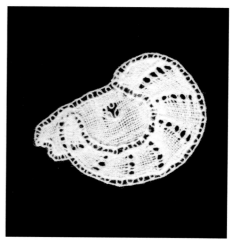

Brooch for a 21st Birthday

Gerlinde Simon   Germany

Bobbins: 11 pairs for edge
          5 pairs for the numbers
Thread: 50/2 linen for edge
          140/2 for the numbers

The edge

Nine repeats of the pattern will, when the
passive pair is pulled, gather the strip into a
round shape with a circumference of the button
mould selected. This movement is carried out
on the pillow before it is joined. This posy is
sewn, with invisible thread, to the edge of
the covered button.

The numbers

On completion sew these in the centre of the
brooch with invisible thread.

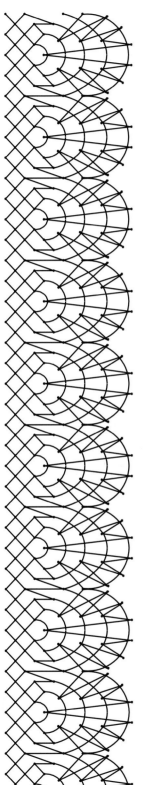

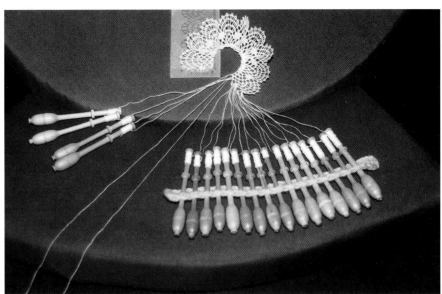

3 2 1 1 1 1 2

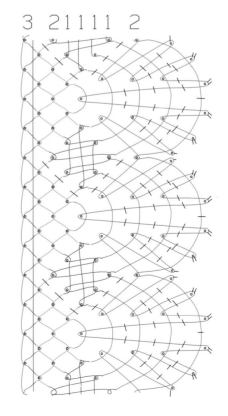

18th, 25th and 40th Birthday Coasters

Bridget M. Cook   UK

These coasters are made in two sections. Make
the outside first.

Outside

Bobbins: 14 pairs
Thread: 70 Egyptian cotton

Complete this outside ring. Then sew in as
needed for the inner number section.

Inner number section

Bobbins: 39 pairs
            gimp pairs as required
Thread: 70 cotton
            No.12 cotton perlé Egyptian
            for the gimps

On completion sew out all pairs
into the inner edge of the
outside frame.

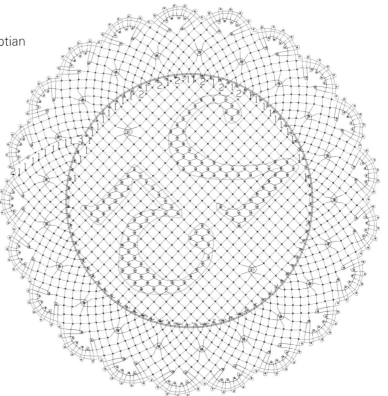

50 and Not Out Cake Mat

Bridget M. Cook   UK

Bobbins: 37 pairs
          3 pairs of gimps
Thread: 60/2 Fresia linen
          Gold gimp thread (Twilley's
          Goldfingering)

There are eight repeats of the pricking to make
the complete mat.

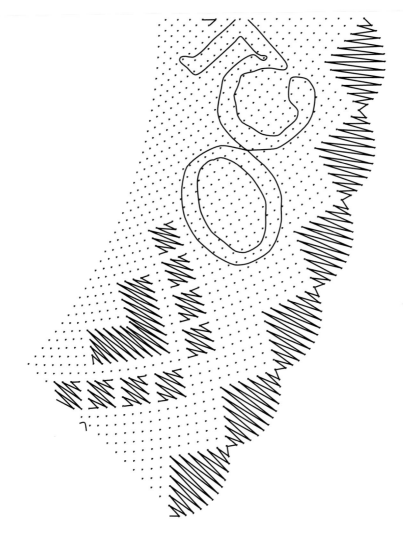

26

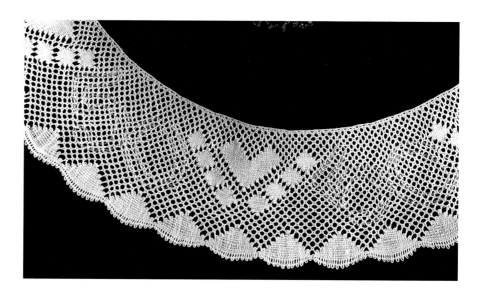

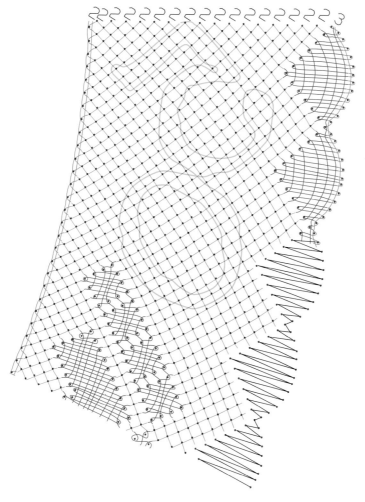

30th Anniversary Handkerchief Corner

Bridget M. Cook   UK

Bobbins: 37 pairs
   Gimps as required

Thread: 30 cotton Broder machine
   cotton perlé no.8 for the gimp

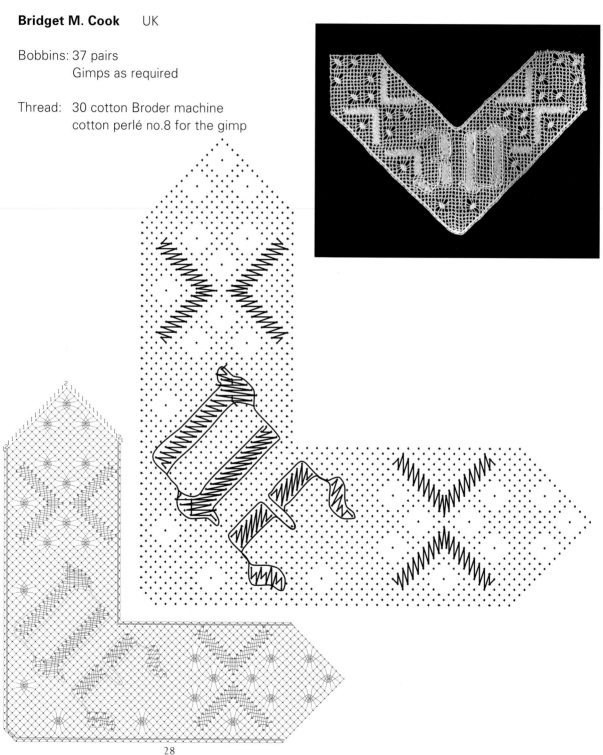

Capricorn Table Coaster

Dorothy McComb   New Zealand

Bobbins: 29 pairs
Thread: 120/2 linen

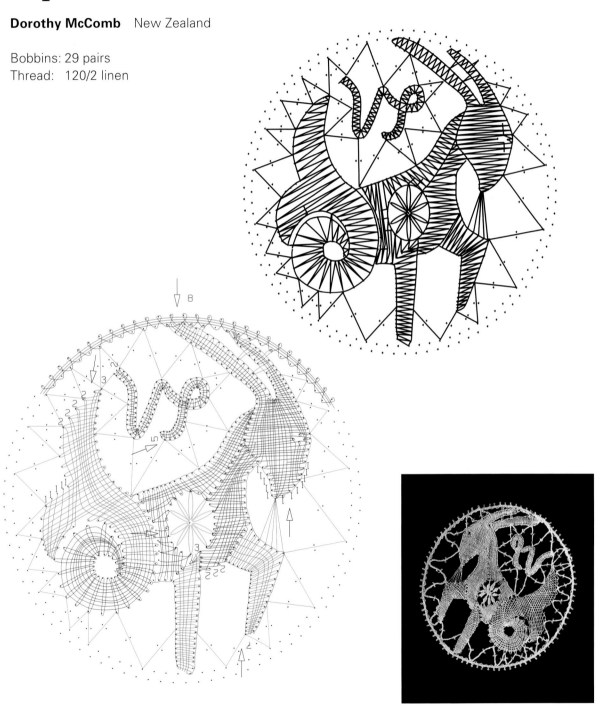

Sagittarius Picture

Radmila Zuman   USA

Thread: 40 cotton

Work each lettered section in turn.

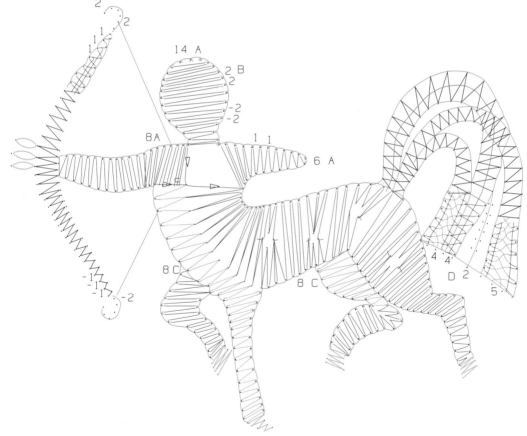

A Quarter Century Of Love

Jeanette S.J. van Ord   Holland

Bobbins: 28 pairs
          1 gimp pair
Thread: 60/2 linen
          Silver thread for the gimp (Twilley's
          Silverfingering)

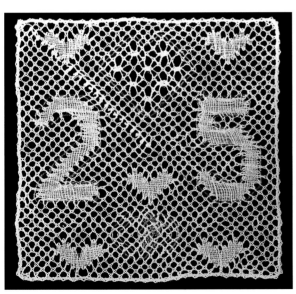

Life Begins at Forty Cake Band

Lesley Thomas   UK

Bobbins: 38 pairs in white
       2 pairs in gold plus 1 pair in gold for
       each pattern repeat
Thread: 100/2 linen
Gold thread: DMC gold, fil d'or
Beads: Small gold beads, 44 for each repeat

Make sufficient repeats to overlap the cake
circumference. Mount on a ribbon of your
choice.

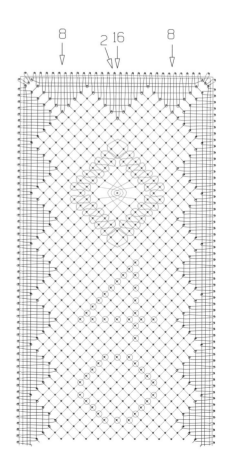

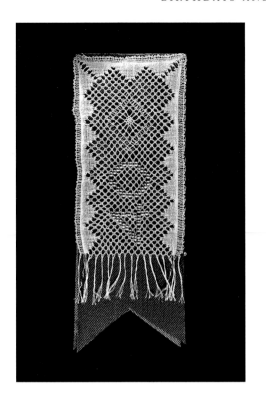

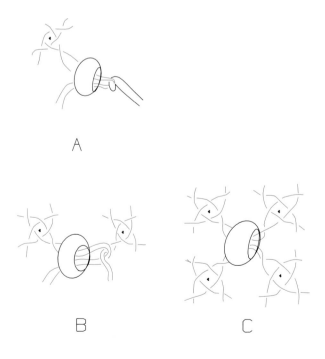

A

B   C

21st Birthday Presentation Handkerchief

Pat Milne   Australia

Torchon
Bobbins: 18 pairs
            1 gimp pair
Thread: 50 DMC Broder machine
            8 DMC Cotton perlé for the gimp

Dieppe ground: halfstitch, pin, halfstitch
and twist

25th and 50th Birthday Motifs

Gil Dye   UK

Bobbins: 8 pairs
Thread: Silver or gold thread - Stephen
          Simpson's lurex, gold or silver, or
          coloured 40 DMC cotton
          cordonnet special

Start at the scroll with a false picot. This forms
the two workers. The remaining pairs are laid
across the pillow. Both sides of the main braid
are worked together. Only four pairs are taken
round the numbers. Pairs are discarded at
the point.

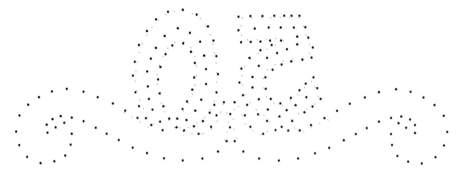

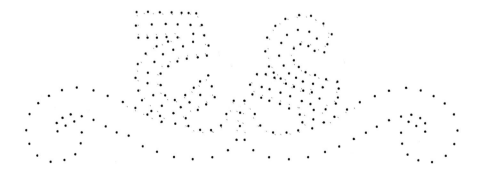

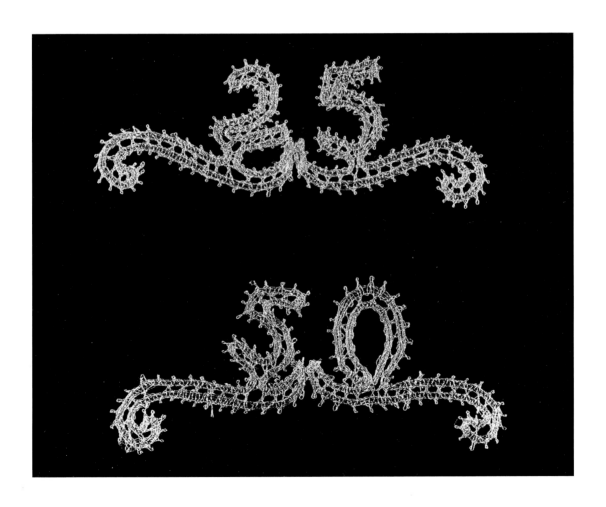

Picture Frame

Gil Dye   UK

Bobbins: 12 pairs
Thread: Metallic thread - 6 Madeira gold,
          or Stephen Simpson's lurex thread

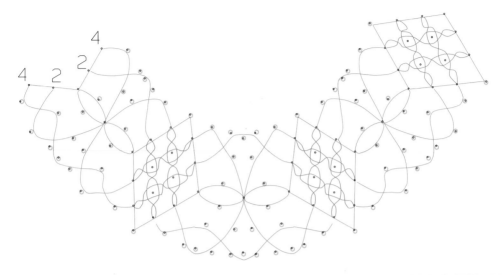

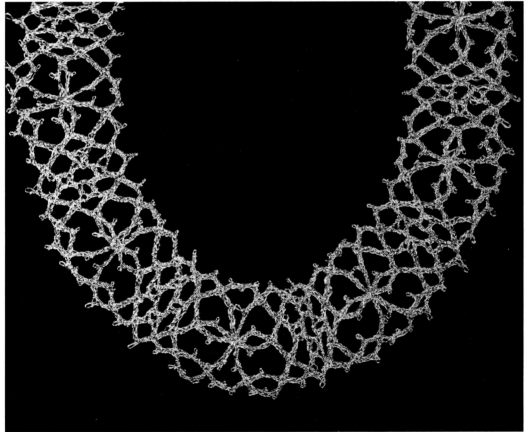

Table Coasters

Helene Schou   Denmark

Scorpio

Thread: 60/2 linen

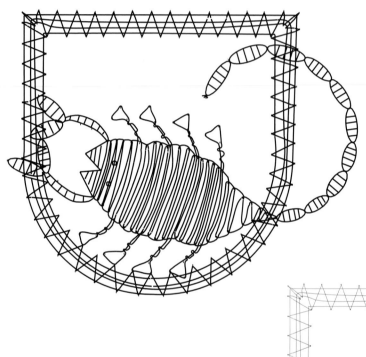

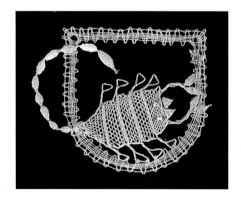

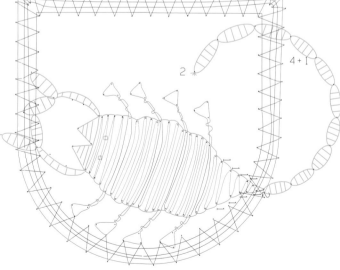

Pisces

Thread: 60/2 linen

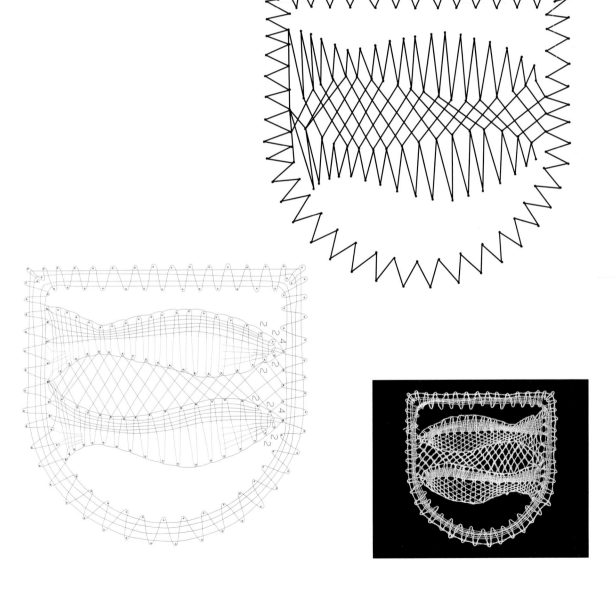

Gemini

Thread: 60/2 linen

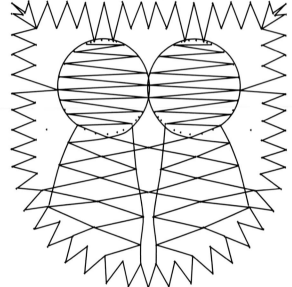

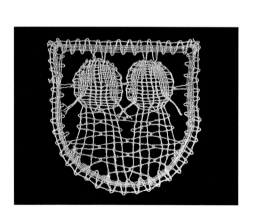

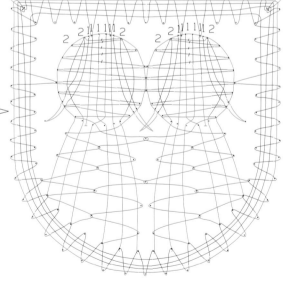

Capricorn

Thread: 60/2 linen

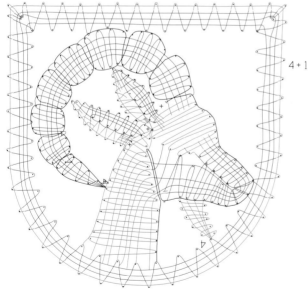

4 + 1

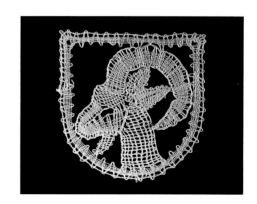

Pisces Cravat

Inge Skovgaard   Denmark

Bobbins: 21 pairs for a single fish
           22 pairs for a fish and tie worked
           together
           13 pairs for the tie strip alone
Thread: 60/2 Bockens linen

This cravat is best made in two sections. Start at
the mouth of the fish and work up the fish and
tie to half-way. Repeat this so that the join of
two sections will be positioned at the back of
the neck.

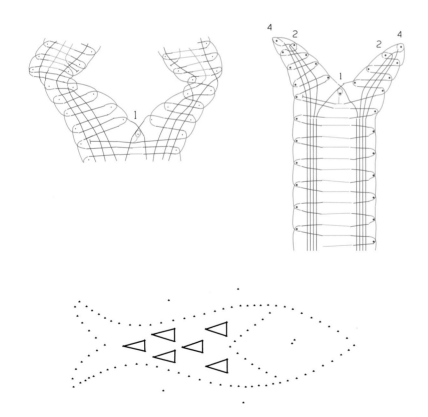

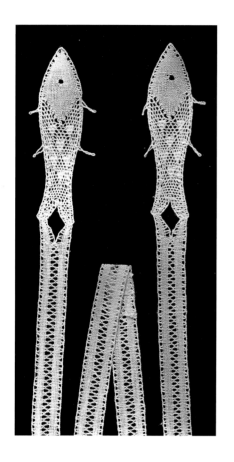

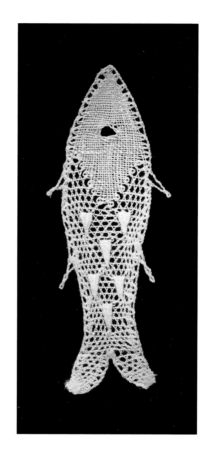

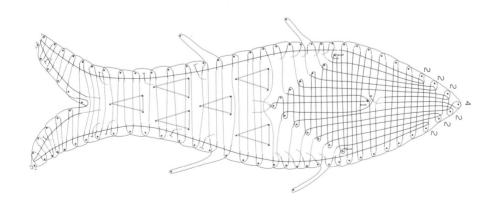

Sources of information

UNITED KINGDOM

The Lace Guild
The Hollies
53 Audnam
Stourbridge
West Midlands DY8 4AE

OIDFA
Tamara Golding
'Nonsuch Too'
27 Ollands Road
Reepham
Norfolk
NR10 4EL

**The British College
of Lace**
21 Hillmorton Road
Rugby
Warwickshire CV22 5DF

International Old Lacers
Ann Keller
Cool Valley
Abingdon Park
Shankill
Dublin

The Lacemakers' Circle
20 Ulverscroft Road
Loughborough
Leicester
LE11 3PU

The Lace Society
Lynwood
Stratford Road
Oversley, Alcester
Warwickshire B49 6PG

Ring of Tatters
Miss B. Netherwood
269 Oregon Way
Chaddesden
Derby DE21 6UR

AUSTRALIA

Australian Lace Guild
National Committee
Box Hill
Victoria 3128

Australian Lace
Magazine
P.O. Box 609
Manly
NSW 2095

BELGIUM

OIDFA
Alice de Smedt
Welvaartstraat 149
B 9300 Aalst
Alg. Spaar-en-Lijfentekas

Belgische
Kantorganisatie
Irma Boone
Gentse Steenweg 296
B-9240 Zele

FRANCE

OIDFA
Suzanne Puech
3 Chemin de Parenty
F-69250 Neuville sur
Saône

GERMANY

OIDFA
Uta Ulrich
Papenbergweg 33
D-32756 Detmold

Deutscher
Klöppelverband
e.V
Schulstr. 38
D-52531
Übach Palenberg

Klöppelschule
Nordhalben
Klöppelschule 4
D-96365 Nordhalben

THE NETHERLANDS

OIDFA
Elly De Vries
Couwenhoven 52-07
NL-3703 ER Zeist

LOKK
Boterbloem 56
NL-7322 GX Apeldoorn

SWITZERLAND

**Fédération de
Dentellières**
Suisses
Evelyne Lütolf
Buhnstrasse 12
CH-8052 Zürich

USA

OIDFA
Elaine Merritt
5915 Kyburz Place
San José CA 95120

International Old Lacers
Editor
Julie Hendrick
2737 NE 98th
Seattle WA 98115

**Point Ground Tours &
Publications**
124 W. Irvington Place
Denver
Co 80223-1539

OIDFA

(International Bobbin
and Needle
Lace Organization)

President
Lydia Thiels-Mertens
Jagersberg 1
B-3294 Molenstede-
Diest
Belgium

Vice President
Alice De Smedt
Welvaartstraat 149
B 9300 Aalst
Belgium